Reavealing a White Lie

Faith vs. Fact

by
Lloyd C. Ford II

Onney Publishing & Performances, Inc.

Copyright © 2018
Lloyd C. Ford, II

ISBN-13: 978-0-9973128-6-7
ISBN-10: 0-9973128-6-6
LCCN: 2018952828

Onney Publishing & Performances, Inc.
P.O. Box 309
Missouri City, Texas 77459
www.onney.net

RIGHTS RESERVED:
Without limiting the rights under the copyright reserved above, no part of this publication may be reproduced, stored in or introduced into a retrieval system, or transmitted in any form or by any means (electronic, mechanical, photocopying, recording or otherwise), without prior written permission of both the copyright owner or the above publisher of this book.

PUBLISHERS NOTE:
The scanning, uploading and distribution of this book via the Internet or via any other means without the permission of the publisher is illegal and punishable by law. Please purchase only authorized electronic editions, and do not participate in or encourage electronic editions, and do not participate in or encourage electronic piracy of copyrighted materials. Your support of the author's rights is appreciated.

PREFACE

"If you can control a man's thinking, you do not have to worry about his actions. When determining what a man shall think, you do not have to concern yourself about what he will do. If you make a man feel that he is inferior, you do not have to compel him to accept an inferior status, for he will seek it himself. If you make a man think that he is justly an outcast, you do not have to order him to the back door. He will go without being told; and if there is no back door, his very nature will demand one." –*Carter G. Woodson*

This book examines the author's background experiences from childhood to adulthood inside the life of Christianity. He attempts to give the reader an inside look of growing up in religious surroundings, and how it influenced his decisions and guided his life. He is challenged to question everything previously learned about religious history and begin to search for the truth. This book puts on trial the concept of faith vs fact, and gives examples of places, events, and other religious beliefs in history where we have been misled. He gives examples in his own life that examine the existence of faith or the perseverance of a man in search of his place in life;

you can be the judge. He also contends with the thought that religious leaders have captured the minds of the people with no serious intent to change the environment they are in, thus, creating a state of inferior circumstances for the very people the church is supposed to serve.

TABLE OF CONTENTS

THE BEGINNING	1
MY LIFE	5
THE EVIDENCE	38
UNDRESSING THE LIE	52
THE MIX UP OF HISTORY	58
WHAT DO WE DO WITH JESUS?	67
WHERE DO WE GO FROM HERE?	78

The Beginning

I struggled over the title for this book; I wanted to choose something that wouldn't offend and turn off the people I am trying to reach before they could even grasp the message I plan to cover. I believe there are few things in this world people hold on to and no matter the circumstance or opposition raised, we cannot bring ourselves to hold these same things in contempt when the light of truth is brought upon it. These things are what we spend most of our lives coveting and those things are our families, our religions, and the universal language of money. I guess it would be a little hypocritical of me not to start this off without raising the question that I think should be asked when writing on a subject such as this. And of course, I'm sure others would ask this while reading something filled with a person's opinion with a lot of facts sprinkled on top.

Who am I to even comment on the topics we are about embark on? Well, the first thing I will point out is that I am a black man in America, which alone has shaped a lot of my family values, religion, and my take on money. I can honestly say I found my purpose, or I rather say realize it, when I woke up to a Donald Trump victory in the 2016 Presidential Election. It made me see that our individual accomplishments would not be enough to push the masses of black people over the top. I want to say I wasn't surprised, but deep down I was. Not because I thought there was no racism or any other excuse Americans tell themselves, but by the amount of hatred gathered in opposition over a Black President who I hate to say had no intent on changing the economic status of black people in this country.

I must add the distrust of the Clintons definitely played a big role in the election of Trump, but mainly a white lash from white America because things had gone far enough. That election brought me a spirit enhanced to do everything in my power to uplift, empower, and expose the truth to black people in every facet of our lives. I was one of the lucky ones that I had a powerful father figure in my life. I always knew I was a winner and had a plan for myself, but what about the rest of the race?

A wise man once said, "No man can ever rise above the conditions of his people." Suddenly it was not enough for my solo act to continue, or even be the main focus, for that matter. I began to view winning differently. It wasn't enough that only my family and I would succeed. I needed to switch from golf, one of the all-time solo sports which focuses on individual accomplishments, to the all-time favorite team sport in America, football (although I'm currently still not watching because of the protest started by Colin Kaepernick to protest the unjust brutality of black people by the police and not a protest against our nation's flag or armed forces).

My mind became consumed with actions to take in order to lift up an entire race to a status, not beholden to anyone for our accomplishments and future economic success. I am not naïve or ego driven enough to think so many others before me didn't try to solve some of the same issues still plaguing us up to this day, but I do feel that we have a unique opportunity in this day and time. We are in the Information Age, and the unique opportunity we have that past generations didn't have is communication. The ability to reach more like-minded individuals through the use of technology is at our fingertips at all times. Before the widespread of the internet, it was impossible to reach a large number of people without being famous, having a lot of money, or being exposed to the correct platforms. This could prove extremely difficult, especially when black.

That being said, this is not the case today, so how are we using our newfound voices to connect and push our communities forward? Are we telling our truth? Or the truth? Should we be using this platform to seek the change we have so long deserved? Or to be accepted in this so-called American dream?

My Life

I will start this off by saying I grew up and remained in the church for the majority of my life, just like every other black family from the south. Before integration and the idea of "you can be whatever you put your mind to", racial equality in the black community gave our children few choices for role models. The bulk of young black boys and girls had to look up to preachers, teachers, and pimps because they were the most common role models.

They were the examples of succeeding black folks during that time, according to my dad, and the most noticeable role models in the black community. My childhood began in the church mainly because my grandfather was a pastor; naturally I had been told my entire life that it was destined for me to follow in the same footsteps. I am now an honest believer that if you are told something long enough, you will start to believe it, despite all of the counter feelings and resistance you put forth.

During my early years, I was made to wake up early, put on my pre-planned outfit, and head to Houston's north side for early morning service, full of loud singing and organs playing. This was a time in my life I rarely understood what was going on, and I can't say that I ever really cared. But I will contribute that to me being a kid, and outside of video games and sports, I didn't care for much. I was a kid, and my prize possessions were my Gameboy, my collection of Pokémon cards, and whatever else kids cared about at that time.

Let me back up and say my dad was heavy into the Bible; I'm talking about knowing scriptures back and forth like the best of them. So many times while in service at church, the preacher would begin to read verses from the Bible, and the most popular ones I would repeat in my head in my dad's voice, as he would do throughout my life. Afterwards, I always came home and told my dad there was nothing new that I learned that he had not already taught me. My dad did not attend service with us due to his dislike and distrust of all Baptist pastors, with the exclusion of my Grandfather. He always wiggled out of church using the Good Book and occasionally quoting 1 Corinthians 3:16, "...knowing you not that you are the temple of God, and that the spirit of God dwells in you."

Each time he would phrase it as a question as if he was asking if I knew that, knowing in his mind he had told me this on many occasions. Plus he wasn't big on giving away money he had earned into a collection plate that he felt was lining the pockets of someone he could beat in a Bible debate 'with both hands tied behind his back'. I'm sure he felt the money was not going to good use. He was no nonsense when it came to those three things I mentioned earlier: religion, his family, and his money.

My dad was a money-making, Bible scripture-quoting, family-providing son of a gun, using his words of course. I owe a lot of my religious knowledge to him in part because of the long talks he felt a father and son were supposed to have. I, being young and hard headed, as folks say, halfway listened but retained more than him and I would know. You will hear a lot of references to my dad throughout this section of the book because he played a major role in my life. Around my middle school ages, I hit a milestone I guess because I began to be forced into this thing my mom called participation. At this time, I was no longer able to sit out in the crowd and wonder carelessly without drawing attention. I found myself participating in the youth choir, even with the lack of bass in my voice. This wasn't the first time I had been in a choir, just the most recent.

This wasn't something I would do fully by choice because of one reason, I could not sing. I quickly learned that being able to sing was not an enforced requirement, not to mention how I felt when I found out we had to come in during the week to practice.

As a kid, I had to receive information in certain ways, or I just didn't get the memo, to put it in simpler terms. If I didn't want to do it in the first place, then my mind shut off instantly. I learned to enjoy some of the times I spent talking too loud just to be 'ssshhed' continuously throughout the church service; I'm beginning to think it was one big joke because none of us could sing, yet the audience never seemed to mind. The singing part of the service had always been my favorite, and I mean the listening part because like I said, I was a horrible singer.

Anyone that has been to a black church knows there's a few things you are guaranteed to see: someone 'catching the Holy Ghost', a huge call to prayer at the altar, and a preacher's call for offering. At my church that sounded something like, "Malachi 3:10. Bring ye all the tithes into the storehouse, that there may be meat in mine house, and prove me now here with, said the Lord of host, if I will not open you the windows of heaven, and pour you out a blessing, that there shall not be room enough to receive it." That scripture was a weekly ritual. The pastor's name was Pastor Lewis, and I am comfortable saying he was the one my dad despised the most over the years; he would be one of the first, but not the last. Now that I am older, I sort of get why Pastor Lewis rubbed my dad the wrong way.

From the designer shades in the pulpit, the city slicker voice he used during the scripture I stated earlier during church offerings, or maybe it was just the fact he had to wake up on the only day of the week he took off to dress up. After going to two separate churches with that same pastor, I guess the Lord finally spoke to my mom and told her it was time for a change. Just like that we were off to the next congregation; it was that simple. I believe it began with the tragic car crash my uncle was involved in; he was my dad's brother. His memorial service had been at the church we would be attending shortly after, and it was the first church we had attended on our side of town.

At the new church, even though my knowledge of religion grew, the connection of emotion that made people jump around, speak in tongues, and cry after receiving extra prayer at the altar just didn't correlate with me.

I was older, around the ninth grade at the time, and I wasn't as brave as I once was to ask someone the hard questions. Why was this? Why wasn't I feeling those anointed feelings? Years back I would have been able to ask the hard questions like I once had with my dad in my younger years.

I asked things like, "Who are God's parents?" After what I would consider an inadequate answer, I followed up with, "How is he just here?" The next answer I would not find satisfying either, but out of fear of a whooping, I wouldn't push much harder. Like I said, religion was one of those things you didn't question. Let's call the new church C.O.G.I.C. During my time there, it was a different experience than I was used to at church; it was more upbeat and with more kids, always an appealing quality for youth. It was more kid-oriented with events and the famous children's church, which gave kids and young adults a place to hang-out while the grown-ups were in the regular church service. Even the grown-ups seemed nicer, some more than others, but I guess my expectations were low. Not because the other churches were bad, but just a little stiffer since the average age at the old church was maybe around 65.

My level of optimism for the new church was high, which I can't explain, but I will contribute it to one of my dad's favorite scriptures, Matthew 17:20, "If ye have faith as a grain of mustard seed, ye shall say onto this mountain..." that's only part of it, but you get the point. After a few bad experiences and with the backing of my dad, I decided I didn't want to attend anymore, and my mom accepted it reluctantly, mainly on the grounds it just didn't look good as the example for my two younger sisters. I can't tell you exactly how long I was gone, but I remember the reason I came back around my 10th grade year was because my cousin had insisted on me coming just to see some girl that he was checking out. Little did I know, she would become my next girlfriend.

I had returned the following Sunday service, but my cousin did not show up for whatever reason, and while shaking hands and giving half hugs, I couldn't help but wonder would I finally find out who this girl was. After greeting everyone familiar, I decided to see what they had in the vending machines since I never ate breakfast. Yet I wanted to avoid that area of the church because an earlier service was finishing up and the hallway tended to get packed. As my stomach growled and I made my way towards the machines, I had a crisp one dollar bill 'burning a hole in my pocket'.

As I got in front of the machines, another wave of people made their way out of children's church; I quickly stood aside and at that moment I saw her. The wave of people poured through the hallway and we locked eyes, and at that moment I knew who my cousin had spoken of, and we would date for about two years.

I only mentioned that story to show I reentered the church, not for the best of reasons, but most of all a girl. Don't get me wrong during my time away from church, the Bible training from my dad didn't stop, with daily quizzes on the rides to and from school. He quoted this stuff daily and I tried not to make a face that said, "I've heard this story a million times." I must admit the information I received did give me a sense of comfort during my time in church. I think it just established the confidence I had in my dad; it was like making an 'A' on a test when I could complete his sentences of whatever Bible verse he was quoting. One thing I did pick up on from year to year inside of the church is that we went over the same verses and stories. Why is that?

We surely didn't cover the entire Bible; we only covered the major stories we all knew even if you spent minimal time within the church. After about the 10th grade, there was nothing new being taught. I want the reader to remember this point for reasons I will get into later. During the time at this new church C.O.G.I.C., I rejoined the choir. It would be referred to as the youth choir ranging from middle school ages all the way to students in college. This time I joined on my own free will. I was trying to increase my chances to see my girlfriend since we didn't attend the same school, and I intended to make use of the one day during the week for practice, and of course, Sundays.

Like I said, this church was a lot more upbeat than all of our previous churches. Most likely that was due to the majority of millennials in attendance. I saw a lot more 'catching the Holy Ghost', running up and down the aisles, and speaking in tongues, which I think is a part of the experience. I have never really felt that feeling in that way. I have always prayed and felt a calming feeling or sensation that cannot be explained, so maybe this is what other people are feeling, just more intense. It amazed me that this was happening with not only adults, but kids as young as 10 years old!

Once, they decided to round all the kids up for some grand showing, for whatever guest we had visiting that particular Sunday. I got a few unholy stares when I politely declined to join the other teens at the altar for extra prayer, but my dad had already gave me permission to decline, respectfully because they were still my elders.

On the second hand, I just wasn't feeling it; I tried to avoid that part of service because I was never into the public showing. I felt it was very unlikely that kids that were younger than me were catching the spirit and they could barely even read. I could come up with the conclusion that they were only imitating what they had been seeing their entire life. I hung out with these kids, and they didn't seem or do anything of significance in their spare time.

I began to think maybe they had more insight or information on the subject, but I quickly ruled that out because we spent most of our time in the back of the church talking about whatever drama was going on at that time. During Sunday school class, I got a good idea of how much everyone knew about the bible. As for Bible data, polls say that around 70% of church goers have not read the Bible, and only around 10% have read the entire book, according to the Huffington Post and other recent studies.

Just those figures alone show most of us get our religious knowledge and understanding from someone else; during my church days, those were not things on my mind. If we were not taking this book seriously enough to read it for ourselves, how could one be mad at someone doubting its validity? At the most recent church, there were a lot of out-of-town events, not to mention in-town events, where the same stories and Bible quotes were shared. We would skip out sometimes and not draw too much attention to ourselves.

This became a yearly routine of planned events, and I could only think, is anyone actually getting something from this or did they just need an event to highlight some so-called accomplishments and best outfits? During these events I did enjoy my time in new places, but like I said, I really didn't get anything out of it. All of the teaching and talking my dad did was not only for me, but my friends, people around the neighborhood, and whoever else he came across. He sought to bring everyone deliverance through being a Christian, and by his good works and teachings. Romans 12:21, "Be not overcome of evil, but overcome evil with good." All the while every church I attended was surrounded by what the church would consider lost souls, drug selling / consumption, and excessive poverty. This didn't stop people in the audience from "whooping and hollering" to the same people that were already getting the message; right outside the walls, there were a lot of people that needed help anyway. I guess the point of religion is to seek out the people in need and try to bring them to the light of God, but instead, all we see today is the saved preaching to the saved.

    I heard someone say something interesting one day in passing and it really made me think; they said, "Black people make the church the center of their community and white people make the bank theirs." This made a lot of sense to me because all the old folks I heard always quoted stuff like, "God will provide." That's a good notion, but the Bible also says, James 2:17: "Faith without works, is dead." In all my years, I had never once seen my church do anything to make a long sustainable change, or any change for that matter, within its own community. Crackheads, alcoholics, and any other individuals making bad decisions, or simply not saved, literally sat in front of the Pastor's entrance.

So from the first minute he pulled in until the last person left, no attempt was made to help them. My guess is that's because they didn't have anything to offer the church. Throughout this time at the church, I saw businesses close, the neighborhood housing decline due to gentrification, and the misfortune continue. I must admit during the time of my attendance these issues rarely crossed my mind in great extent. I was still young, and I'm sure my mind was still on girls, and according to my dad, they should be because he always said I would have my entire life to worry about grownup things. The rest of my high school years especially during my senior year, I really ramped up my praying; now that I sit back and think about it, I had a lot going on. I was starting on the varsity football team, trying to fulfill my lifelong dream of going to college on a scholarship, and I still needed to take the SAT, not to mention other teen drama.

I remember around that time being my 12th grade year, I was beginning to take things more serious by actually reading the Bible on the starter program, where you read a portion each day until the end of the year. I had never even said a cuss word out loud but on occasion; I thought that was sort of weird, but I took a sense of pride when it came to being different. Being independent and stubborn has been a part of me; sometimes it has served me well. I began to pray every day to be better, make better grades, and hope I got that football scholarship because I really didn't have a plan B.

I prayed that I could live up to the expectations I put on myself to become half the man my dad was for our family. Something I made sure I suppressed was any weakness and any doubts, and did this always work? Of course not. My dad and I had a great relationship, but he was not was a shoulder to cry on. We were more of the 'men don't cry' tribe unless under extreme circumstances like a death in the family.

I'm not saying he would not have embraced me as he has in certain situations, but those were emotions seldom needing to be displayed. I was used to pushing all signs of weakness deep down and keeping it moving to my next goal. Around this time, I didn't have a girlfriend anymore, so my main focus was on sports and trying to graduate school. Then again, girls never really left my mind because

I was a teenage boy. Back to the important stuff, my faith in the Bible gave me a silent sense of confidence. Back in the day when I played running back on the football team, the coach would judge me solely on my size; I was only 130 lbs.

At the time, all I could think about was that I was the only one stepping up. We were going against the varsity and they were a lot bigger, so they would just grab the next poor soul to throw to the lions.

I reference these stories to make a point of the Bible-instilled confidence I didn't know I had in myself. I would always repeat the scripture in my head, Ecclesiastes 9:11: "The race is not always given to the swift nor the strong but he who endures until the end." I started to get that feeling once you put your trust in God for so long, your prayers finally start to come true. I thought to myself, "This is what real Christians must feel like," in a joking manner. I went from getting pushed to the sidelines to finally starting as wide receiver. I could have just basked in how my life was going and not gave anything else much thought, but I didn't. I began to think deeper into what got me where I was. Was it my belief in God and myself?

Was it the hard work I put in during the off season, or was it just life's circumstances? I would like to think my hard work had a lot to do with it, but I feel if there's one person you need to be real with, that's yourself. I would always wonder what happened to all of the guys that I grew up with that played the same positions as I did. Did I just beat them out for the starting spot? Did I work hard over time and become more talented? In most cases I would have said I was starting by condition; I will get to how I came to that perception. Most of the guys I played with in my early years of high school that started were some of the most talented players I would ever play with. Some had beards and were more mature, along the lines the coaches were looking for. Some of them were naturally bigger, faster, and stronger. But over an entire football season a lot could happen because of rules like "no pass, no play".

That rendered a lot of players ineligible since bad behavior got them kicked out of school and issues could be going on at home; this was the hood. I saw a lot of my teammates over the years disappear because of the reasons I just mentioned. The question I asked myself is would I be in the same position and awarded the same opportunities if those guys hadn't fallen by the wayside for whatever reason. Some of those guys had pro-like ability even in middle school; we won our first football game without ever putting on full pads until the day of the game, undefeated and unscored upon, but that was in the 7th grade.

Once we entered high school, I think the system made it harder for young black boys to make it out untouched, and not just the boys; there was a full system to keep black people in a permanent state of poverty through our educational system. I will get a little more into that later.

By my 10th grade year, more of our starting athletes had fallen off due to academic performance. Skipping class was something else I didn't do because I could never think of anywhere to go, and the remaining would move up to varsity after the coaches had seen them dominate in a few freshman or junior varsity games. Let's not forget what brought me here: my prayers and faith in God along with my hard work during the summer. Or was it simply because those guys couldn't stay out of trouble and pass their classes?

To make the story short, I choose to think it was a combination of them all. I didn't want anyone to fail in order for me to get a chance, but that's exactly what happened. If they would have been just halfway good students, would I have ever touched the field? At this point who knows, but I will say my trust in my religion had kept me afloat. I did realize there were other factors in that scenario on why so many black kids from inner city schools with world class talent never make it out of the hood. The moral of the story is those situations helped me take a look at how my religious views shaped a lot of the views I had, but I guess that's what it is designed to do.

I finished out my senior year and got a football scholarship to a school in Bismarck, North Dakota. I came to the conclusion my prayers had been answered practically enough. Of all of the schools out there, I attended a Catholic one, and the environment was different because it was majority white. Every school I had attended prior had been at least 90% black. This was a new setting, but not an unfamiliar one. One of my childhood friends and I had attended his majority white church frequently growing up; I remember visiting a lot, especially when I wasn't going to the church with my mother and sister.

Visiting there, I got really comfortable being the minority in group settings, but at this particular church, I found myself daydreaming a lot, maybe because I found the lessons even more dull than normal. I was just counting down the minutes until it was time to play basketball, video games, or any other activity that consumed our time. I actually enjoyed that church because the people were a lot nicer than my previous churches, but the singing was so bad, I never made it through a full adult service. What did I really expect? I should have known the type of soul-gospel singing I was used to could not possibly be reproduced there. I didn't think I could be getting prepared for places I would be visiting later on in my life.

Back to my Catholic College, my entire two years there I can't recall seeing a single surveillance camera. Sorry…that's weird to me; I am a black man from the south, and I thought the cops would put cameras in the restroom if they could. After asking one of the staff members why I didn't see any, I found it was simply because it was a religious school and they trusted people. I don't know how true that is, but that wouldn't work where I'm from. I later found out you pump your gas first, then paid for it afterwards and that blew my mind even more; I still wonder sometimes how that system is working for them. While at the college up north, my first class was Theology 101.

Bright and early at 8 am, it would be would be the last class I would take at 8 am the rest of my college years. It proved to be too early for me to wake up for class, particularly since I had the power to choose. I thought we would really dig deep and learn about the Bible, during this class, as well as the people in it, and maybe even about some of the people that actually wrote it. I was wrong! The class turned out to be one long bible study class with homework, and we never got into the information I felt I really wanted to know. We went over Bible verses, but the instructor never talked about the individuals that authored its pages, or the sources they used to make the versions we have today. No outside proof that any of the stories we were learning were factual.

I can honestly say everything they were teaching in that class my dad had already drilled into my mind. The only thing I remember from that class is that it was extremely cold, and me thinking who would want to live up here in the cold, and that this weather wasn't for black people. I spent about 2 years at that college until I began to feel I wasn't receiving the great college experience that my high school classmates were having, according to Facebook pictures and any other ways we stayed current at that time.

I guess I was looking for college to be like all of the movies I had watched with the crazy parties and getting drunk, which I had never done, and it was not nearly as eventful as the movies. Although

I had a lot of fun at times just sitting around drinking, it just wasn't my type of fun, not to mention the freezing weather. At this point in my life, I wasn't a heavy drinker so I always ended up the designated driver, shuttling my friends home from parties. But I enjoyed driving because I didn't actually have a car of my own on normal days. I value my time up north because it gave me a chance to really see how other people live in another region. I would probably never visit outside of college or politics, and it gave me a peek into what shapes other people's views of the world.

The majority of people I came into contact with were of the Catholic faith; I didn't notice this until walking through campus and seeing a black mark on the foreheads of everyone. I never asked anyone why they did that because I was a Christian and that wasn't changing; later, I would find out it was called "Ash Wednesday". Eventually, I will describe my first experience in a Catholic Church.

With all of my childhood questions about God, I had never given much thought into actually researching other religions and what they had to offer. As far as I knew, most religions were geographical. At the time, I think I subconsciously abandoned all of the questions that went unanswered or were so-called controversial; I always got that look of disapproval when the subject needed to change. Once again, my dad was a firm believer of Proverbs 22:6, "Train up a child in the way he should go; even when he is old he will not depart from it." That was just another favorite he quoted frequently.

With him speaking to everyone he came in contact with and no matter the conversation, it always ended up with my dad busting out in scripture, but not in the preachy way that made you look for the first exit. My father had a way that made the Bible fit the circumstances of your life, encouraging others to stay and listen on whatever street corner we were on in the hood. I knew everyone saw the sincerity in his eyes as he spoke.

After those couple of years up north, I was ready to move closer to home because I assumed I was missing out on the real college experience. Near the end of my stay, I realized how much I had prayed, but not once had I been to church. I never really had the desire or transportation to attend any churches in the city, but with my experiences from the past, I figured the churches would be lacking in the part of service I enjoyed most, which was the singing. I had not been invited to church until my final week I spent up north at my roommate's family house, which was a few hours away from campus. His town was so small they had graduation with a total number of around twelve graduates.

I didn't think they still had towns that small, and all I could think next is I wonder how many black people, if any. I mean, face it, where I was at, about 90% of the black people were there for college sports. The adventurous part of being up north is I got to see all of the things they did for fun that we couldn't always enjoy back home like riding on snowmobiles and other snow-involved activities we could find. I finally got that invite to visit a Catholic Church.

Entering the church, I immediately became the object of everyone's stares, as I knew I would, but everyone that actually spoke was pleasant. We would end up sitting about six rows from the front, and as the service began, I saw I wasn't the only black person present; there was an altar boy around the age of 10. I got kind of apprehensive because I didn't see any black parents; I could only imagine if he had been the only black person in the whole town, and mainly on the fact, he would miss out on all of the black experiences of being around people that look like him.

We were seated on the end; my roommate next to me, then his brother and sister, and on the opposite end were his parents. It was around December and schools were out, so the church was particularly full that Sunday, according to my roommate's parents.

Directly in front of us was an old retired school teacher that had to be well into her eighties. We had only been in church for about 30 minutes when it was brought to my attention that she was already nodding off, as in falling asleep. To this day I cannot tell you why that had been so amusing to my roommate and I, but once the chuckles started, they just wouldn't stop. By this time the whole family had caught wind of what we were laughing at, and a minute later, the entire row erupted in laughter.

The only thing I could think about while trying my best not to laugh too hard was what the other members would think when we were disrupting service. Would they think that this is what happens when you let too many black people in the church? (Not Serious) At least I could finally say I checked something off of the list before I left, visiting a Catholic Church before I left since the odds were I wouldn't back home.

Leaving the school up north, I kind of felt a feeling of relief. I would finally be close to home, along with all of my friends I had left behind, but I was still grateful for the experiences I had my couple of years in college. Coming close to home not only meant seeing family, friends, and more fun, but also I would be returning to my home church C.O.G.I.C. like I had never left. I couldn't wait to get home and attend service and receive all of the love and questions about college, as I always did at least twice a year when I came home for the holidays.

I enrolled at Prairie View A & M University to major in Management Information Systems and I began to become more wrapped up in my life, so my church attendance was still not an every week occurrence. My church was about 40 minutes away from campus and the gas sometimes didn't seem worth it, and I was a broke college student. As more time passed, I began to see our church through more mature lenses and started to see a lot more unscrupulous things.

My parents were big believers in kids staying kids without the stress of grownup situations, and we would have our entire life to worry about those things. But, as a result, my sisters and I were not enlightened on all of the issues or problems that may have overwhelmed other families. I feel like overnight I was able to see through any fake smiles, fake preachers, and words of God being quoted by false prophets and replaced with lies, deceit, and greed.

I started paying more attention to the things that were going on around me and began to ask questions to other members around me about some of the things that were going on. Most of the members I spoke with seem to know about the different situations going on around the church, and it seemed to be acceptable behavior. At the least I thought it was seriously unacceptable and I began to get the feeling I could no longer be a part of it. I didn't want to be a part of any phony things going on, and I couldn't turn a blind eye to what was happening around me. I imagine religion to be like the movie *Inside Man*.

The movie began with the robbery of a bank, and during this robbery, the thieves came up with a way to escape that reminds me of characters and events of the Bible. When the robbers first entered, they made the hostages strip down and change into exactly what they were wearing, plus the added blindfolds. They also separated them in about three different rooms in order to further confuse them. When I first saw this movie, I thought they did that to either distance themselves from the hostages or disguise a much greater plan.

This tactic became useful during the interrogation process of the cops after this was all over. Fast forwarding in order to get the point, they did devise a rather genius plan to get the stolen goods out, but you will have to watch the movie for that. The robbers ended up walking out the front doors, or should I say running out with hostages? This was only possible because let's remember everyone was dressed alike, so there was no way for the cops to distinguish between good and bad guys. Still, the thief's road to freedom would not be granted just yet. After the dust had settled and all suspects were rounded up, this is when the lie was injected.

During the interrogations the detectives quickly discovered that since the hostages were blindfolded and separated for hours, none of the hostages could identify a large amount of other hostages, or more importantly, identify who wasn't a hostage. By this time I'm sure you are wondering how this is going to relate to the Bible, but by the hostages having limited knowledge of their surroundings, the robbers were able to take advantage of the situation. The detectives questioned each so-called hostage one by one, but each actual robber would validate the others' false claims of being a real hostage.

This left the cops in an impossible position. By the end of the interrogations, the cops had nothing solid that would point out any obvious suspects, and with no video evidence, they had little to go on; eventually they had to release everyone that had been involved and walked out of the doors of the bank. This part of the movie made me associate it with religion and the Bible since none of the people or stories mentioned in it can be verified with physical proof. The Bible has become so widely known around the world that we all took it to be 100% true. I will present more evidence than just a scene of a movie later on in the book.

At this time in my life, I began to ask the hard questions, and I understand a lot of people were afraid to research this topic because it would be seen as blasphemy or socially unacceptable, especially in the south. I believe we need to question and research everything we have been taught in schools and by the past generations in order to seek the truth. Anyone or anything that tells you that is forbidden can't be something that frees your mind, body, and soul; it's a foundation of control.

Like a wise man once said, "If you are comfortable with my oppression, then you are my oppressor." Anything that condones the slaughtering of innocent children, contradictions on slavery, and allows the justification of evil can't truly be of God. When my journey started and I began to research everything I had formally been taught to believe in, I would still attend church occasionally; the conflict of believing in something all of my life was still inside and would not go away overnight.

I continued to attend because like a lot of people it was a routine I had followed my entire life. Sometimes it just felt wrong being up on a Sunday and not attending church unless there was a good reason. Each time I attended after that, my experience got less enjoyable with every passing hour, and I found myself only staying just long enough to hear the choir. The gospel songs I could still listen to without agreeing fully to their message, but that was normal; there were a lot of rap songs I didn't necessarily agree with either, but I simply enjoyed the music.

Fast forwarding a little bit, Trump had just been elected, and to be honest the shock was still setting in. I really thought he had no chance of winning, but I was wrong, along with a lot of people including the mainstream media. With racial tensions already running high due to police shooting unarmed black men in the streets, a group of us like-minded individuals began to start a group to help combat the issues we decided needed to be addressed.

As the initiative grew, we decided we needed a suitable location to meet and invite others, rather than our apartment complex lobbies with very limited space. I was still going to church at the time, so my first thought was my church since I had spent many nights there for choir practice. It was centered in one of the communities we wanted to help, and of course since I was a long time member, I thought the price factor would weigh in our favor.

It was never in my mind that the church would be opposed to having a meeting that would only benefit the community; my imagination even thought they might be excited and refuse to take any money, but I was swiftly brought back to reality. On my next visit I started to ask around for the person that was in charge of making that decision. With a straight face, the person I won't name expressed that it would be five hundred dollars plus the cost for security just to have a meeting for one hour, even though we only expected around 20 or 30 people. I thought that was jaw dropping because I could rent a real facility with that price, and when it came to security, his reasoning was that it was church policy and they had always done it in the past.

I knew this to be false because years prior when I was in the youth choir spending my Wednesday nights at practice, I don't recall ever seeing security, only the women and children. The closest men we had were us, the teenage boys in the choir itself. This further proved the hypocrisies of the church, and that was my last day setting foot in that church or any church for that matter, even up to this day.

My mother had paid the church thousands of dollars over the years but got nothing in return; she had paid the church enough to carry her a couple of generations I thought. I would also find out that members had been overcharged for weddings and other events typically held in the church by members. There are around 20 black churches in my neighborhood alone but yet they do nothing to fight poverty, drug infestation, gentrification, or support our black owned businesses, yet they rake in millions without giving anything sustainable back. Are they not complicit in the destruction?

Most of the people reading this will agree that all of the things I mentioned are true, but they will be back in the audience of one of those same churches that are part of the problem. The next Sunday you attend a church, keep in mind these are the same individuals that we are convinced God is speaking through. If you see a church that is flourishing and the neighborhood around it is in shambles, I think it is safe to say that church may not be doing the right thing.

I began to use Sundays as my research day; I woke up early and thought about all of the things they would have been talking about in church that morning. I did not discourage my wife from going if that's what she wanted because we all have the right to believe in whatever we want. But as a result of all of the new information I was learning, I had to share it with someone, so she would be the main soundboard that heard all of my new discoveries.

In my opinion, there is overwhelming evidence in opposition to a lot of the things in the Bible. I didn't seek out to change her mind, but be the spark or light bulb rather to motivate her to seek the truth for herself. Fear blinds people to the truth and, "Christianity has become a mental safe place for black people that don't study who they are," said best by Cory Holcombe. I have realized in my fight for the best for my people, we have to be humble in our aspirations, grateful in our success, and resilient in our failures.

I never wanted to be one of those people that only discussed religion and annoyed all of the people around me. My intentions were to state the facts when the moment presented itself, ideally at a time when someone works up the courage to bring it up because religion is becoming one of those topics you don't really discuss in public places, even amongst friends. You will hear me say this multiple times throughout this book, but my goal here is not to debate interpretation of the verses, but to point at the lack of historical facts inside of its text. Hopefully it sparks that light bulb in you to do the research of your own and discover the truth.

If we know the Bible was written by man and we all agree man is not perfect, then it would be naïve of me to think after thousands of years man would not have changed it for monetary or personal gain. If you agree with that statement, then your research should start today.

The Evidence

This topic can start at many points in time, but I will start with the development of the literature that got us our Bible. You will see me refer to B.C.E. for 'Before Common Era' instead of B.C. and C.E. for 'Common Era' instead of A.D. because less scholars are subscribing to the mainstream life and death timeline abbreviations. It began in 325 C.E. at the Council of Nicea, often regarded as the first council for the church; around 118 bishops were in attendance.

All of these bishops came together in one place in order to vote on what books should be included into the Bible and other major things that they added by vote and not by a divine vision. This council lasted around two months and twelve days, and during this time is when Jesus was declared to also be God and for the first time in history, be a real man too.

It is important to note that before this council, the name Jesus wasn't found in any religious text, but the common term "Christ" was used and researchers took this as a shortening of his name. I don't believe this to be the case, and I will address this more in later chapters. Just that little bit of information made me want to know more and it peaked my interest. I searched further, and they weren't finished yet. The so-called leadership called another council named the "First Council of Constantinople" which was named after Constantine and held 56 years later in 381 C.E. Around 150 bishops were in attendance and they discussed the Holy Spirit being also God. They also developed "Pneumatology", which is the study of the Holy Spirit, the very thing they just created.

This information is no secret and you can literally google this stuff to get the same answers; this made me realize that a lot of the information I regarded to as godly had been brought us by way of vote. I had many questions regarding the things that I was discovering, for example: what was the Holy Spirit before they put it to a vote? Was the Holy Spirit around before this time? Who gave them the right to add it? This was the second council that had changed something significant in the Bible that I thought was always there. First the creation of Jesus being man and God, and now creating the Holy Spirit; what would be next? I didn't expect the changes to stop at this point and they didn't. 50 years later in 431 C.E., around 200 bishops came together to form the "Council of Ephesus".

The additions of this council would be something that we all still refer to even today. Called the Triune Doctrine, commonly referred to as the Holy Trinity, the council also decreed that Mary is Jesus' mother. These were bold declarations that they were making. Where were they getting this information from? These are some of the questions I will answer later on in this section. 19 years later in 451 C.E., the last council, the Council of Chalcedon, would take it a little further and proclaim Jesus is truly a human being and God. The first question I asked myself was before this time, was there no earthly Jesus? If there were an earthly Jesus, why did they have to declare that here? I am raising these questions not only to answer them later, but to encourage you (the reader) to again do your own research. Even though this is not common knowledge, it is easily researched. At the Council of Chalcedon, they also intended to close the doors on any more changes that could be made to this doctrine by announcing that no one shall be permitted to produce, write down, or compose any other creed, or to think or teach otherwise. Those who dared to compose another creed or religious doctrine to oppose what had already been created would be "anathematized", which means to be cursed or condemned.

This would ensure the mass population would accept the doctrine that had already been produced to keep them in a permanent state of obedience. The leaders' decision to now all of a sudden make it illegal to write down or teach any other doctrine made it clear to me that this was put in place for control and not to give the masses of people a closer connection to God. All of the changes that had been made to the so-called holy doctrine had been done for power, and not from a divine process like we have all been led to believe.

To say the least, we have been deceived a lot when it comes to the detailed facts of history, and if we had the entire truth, I believe our feelings for them would change. We all know of the holiday St. Patrick's Day but rarely does anyone know the real story behind it, a man named St. Patrick who drove the snakes out of Ireland and defeated the Druids. The history we have been taught, if at all, would tell you this is a day celebrating Christianity and driving the snakes out of Ireland.

What they haven't said is that the Druid snake people that they referred to were the Ancient Kemite spiritual system, which had the Cobra as their symbol. At that time, the people of those lands knew the original spiritual systems came from Egypt and that the Roman Catholic Church had no authority to change it, so they set out to take over those lands and whoever wouldn't go along with the new things they were putting in place.

This happened around the 5th Century C.E. when the Council of Chalcedon declared no one would be able to teach any other religious beliefs, except for the one they were putting in place during the council meetings. Once the Druids referred to as the snake people opposed the changes to the things that they were claiming in the new doctrine, they were sentenced to be anathematized.

This is when St. Patrick was commissioned to drive the Druids still practicing the Ancient Kemite religion from Egypt out of that land, and I don't mean the invaders that inhabit present-day Egypt.

After driving all of the Druids out that didn't agree with their new narrative, the Roman Catholic Church erected over 300 churches to spread their new account for the religion they were trying to shape and mold to fit their vision of what it should be. This is one of the examples I wanted to use because there are many people around the world that celebrate this so-called holiday annually without fully understanding the lightly concealed truths behind its origins. I don't know about anyone else, but knowing these facts and others I have yet to mention has shaped my views on holidays I celebrate today.

They were willing to lie, steal, and kill to push their version of religion that we follow today and a lot of us know this, but yet we will still follow it and believe in its words. The church wanted to make it impossible to follow anything other than what they wanted, and after all of these things were set in place and all other beliefs were banned, the "Dark Ages" would begin, starting in 500 C.E. and lasting nearly a thousand years. The "Dark Ages" were a time the church used to expand their reach on the world and suppress anything that contradicted their point of view.

Historians like Edward Gibbons expressed the corruption of a counterfeit Christianity. Also around this time between 500 C.E. and 1000 C.E., only the priests were allowed to read; this was another tactic used to further suppress and control the flow of information. Let's remember this was the beginning stages of what we now call the King James Version. This is a very brief overview of the most crucial topics I felt I should cover in order for you to get enough background knowledge easily verified by facts of history.

Immediately following the "Dark Age", the "Middle Age" allowed an earlier form of Christianity to go unchallenged for over 500 years; this gave them an advantage on the rest of the world and it would set the ball rolling for what was to come next, the Crusades. The Crusades took place between 1095- 1291 C.E.; this was a direct way of getting rid of whoever didn't go along with their beliefs. They swept around from land to land, partially in response to the Muslim Crusades years before, but that's a topic for another day.

During the Crusades some of the places they fought over were Jerusalem, Turkey, and Syria, just to name a few. The church didn't only have resistance from outside forces to the new details they were inserting into the doctrine; it was heavily opposed from within, causing a split of the Christian church called "The Great Schism". This caused the church to split into the Eastern Orthodox Church and the remaining Roman Catholic Church around 1054 C.E. It was driven by the pursuit of power and not by the divine right given to them by God as they claimed, but rather a practice in information suppression, corruption, and murder.

The Dark Ages were a notable time in history that some of us may have heard about in school, but the real details of the issues were downplayed to say the least, and after the Dark Ages we went into the Renaissance period, called the "Age of Exploration and Discovery". Conventional history will say that the Renaissance period was a time of revival of the teaching and learning of the arts, and the awakening of Roman culture. But it was also a time that the power in charge would now allow the masses of the population to share in the wealth of knowledge.

During the Renaissance period, the most significant movement was called "humanism", which is defined as "a philosophical and ethical stance that emphasizes that value and agency of human beings, individually and collectively, and generally prefers critical thinking and evidence over acceptance of dogma or superstition." This movement was discussed by notable people in history.

For instance, Martin Luther, who lived between 1483- 1546 C.E. and believed that people should have the freedom to read the doctrine for themselves. Among other things, they desired to change with the Bible of that time, not for religious reasons, but for the greed and power of the ones in charge. During this time the Bibles were still being translated and written by hand, and that fact alone concerns me on how many errors that occurred that they were unaware of.

During this period people were finally able to read for themselves after the information suppression period, but still not able to translate the text into other native languages. Individuals like William Tyndale were burned at the stake in 1536 C.E. for translating the Bible to English just to let you know they were serious about the control of information. But the game changer was in 1445 C.E. when the Gutenberg printing press was built; it allowed the books to be produced and spread around quicker than ever before.

During this next time period, they were still making large amounts of modifications to the Bible to boost their spiritual or divine right to riches over the people of the world. The goal was to enslave the minds of normal and easily scared population of that time.

I want the reader to realize these are the same people that we accepted this Bible from and that the version we have today is nothing but a watered-down, corrupted, and man-driven book to keep us in a permanent debate over its false contents and claims. I do believe that the Bible contains valuable information below its surface meanings, but it has been written in a way to manipulate and deceive over the centuries.

Around 1539 C.E. with Henry VIII, the Great Bible was officially translated into the English language for the first time; not long after in 1560 C.E., it would be revised again. The revisions were done by the same authors of The Geneva Bible and also named the Pope the Anti-Christ. The different versions of the Bible were being revised for power to rule, and to go as far as naming the Pope the Anti-Christ says a lot about who they were trying to discredit at that time.

During this time in history, the Bible or religion changed with each new ruler and was fueled by their greed to conquer everything around them. In 1568 C.E., eight years after the Geneva Bible, comes Queen Elizabeth I and The Bishop's

Bible. This particular version had so many issues that by 1572 C.E. it was being revised, and her version was always less desired compared to The Geneva Bible; during her reign, she would kill because of it. The Hampton Court Conference in 1604 C.E. was called by King James who assumed the throne a year earlier, and the reason for this conference was to address all of the issues they had with Queen Elizabeth's version, the Bishop's Bible. They called for a new translation of the scriptures, and they would use the Geneva Bible as their guide, and at the same time still teaching the words of Bishop's Bible to the population.

King James didn't care for the Geneva version of the Bible because it denied the absolute power of kings, known as the Divine Right of Kings. The King James Version, from the time of its development in 1611 C.E. to as late as 1950, has been constantly modified to fit a certain narrative, and that narrative does not have anything to do with finding God, in my opinion. For example, Deuteronomy 28:68 says, "And the Lord shall bring thee into Egypt again with ships, by the way whereof I spake unto thee, Thou shalt see it no more again: and there ye shall be sold unto your enemies for bondmen and bondwomen, and no man shall buy you."

In the original of Deuteronomy, it spoke nothing of slaves going back to Egypt; it was something else put in place to deceive readers that some type of prophecy was being fulfilled when the so called slave trade had begun. While doing this research, I often asked myself questions like, "Why do we believe the people that put the Bible together to have had good intentions? Who gave them the right to make changes from 325 C.E. until the King James Version in 1611?" I am not doubting the existence of God, but simply questioning the stories and false divinity that the Bible claims; I believe we should seek more power from within. In a scene of the latest Star Wars movie, Luke Skywalker was conflicted between the Jedi religions.

He saw the evil that it could produce, even though it was made for good, and he was going to burn the last of the Jedi books so that no one could ever possess them. Before he could go through with destroying them, he got cold feet and paused. While in thought, Yoda appeared and had them struck by lightning and set on fire; Luke stood there surprised. Yoda explained that while those books had great wisdom inside, they meant nothing because the real power came from within. Even the Bible says in 1 Corinthians 3:16-17, "Do you not know that you are God's temple and that God's spirit dwells in you? If anyone destroys God's temple, God will destroy him. For God's temple is holy, and you are that temple."

I believe we should seek the power from within, instead of inside of the pages of a book we know has not been made to benefit mankind, but to fuel the greed of humanity. At some point in time, we have to ask ourselves the hard questions, and no one before us has had the easy access to knowledge as we do right now with the internet, but most refuse to research these types of subjects because they may see it as going against God. We will continue to examine more examples of false doctrine, verses, and books of the Bible that have not been verified by actual evidence of history. This section was intended to give a brief breakdown of how the Bible was assembled from the first "Council of Nicea" up to the present King James Version. Also, I want to point out times in history the Bible was manipulated by man and how fictional characters became real beings over time.

When your beliefs don't coincide with facts, you have been misled. I believe the Bible has great morals to live by, but I think it began to hinder us when we dedicated so much of our time and money to it. We receive nothing tangible from it, and when we believe stories to be literal, like the stories of

Jesus, Moses, or Noah, I believe we begin to get a false representation of history; we lose touch with the real history and accomplishments of the African nation.

As a former Christian, I don't intend to debate your faith or what you feel Jesus has done for you thus far. Once upon a time when I did follow Christianity, I believed that all of my prayers were being answered and Jesus was a growing presence in my life, so I will attempt to stick to the real proven facts of history. I truly believe once people see the enormous amount of faith it takes to believe in some of the details pertaining to the Bible, you may conduct your own research and realize this religion was not made in order to free you, but with the intentions of keeping you in a permanent state of submission.

UNDRESSING THE LIE

Back in ancient times, knowledge of any kind was regarded to as sacred and in the retelling of stories, they passed on valuable information such as seasons, navigation, and other valued knowledge before things were being written down. In the process of writing these stories down, one important word came to mind, 'allegory', which is defined as a story with two levels of meanings.

First, the apparent story with characters and a plot, then there is the symbolic level or deeper meaning; they intended for people to be able to read it but yet still ignorant of its true meaning. I will attempt to display the falsehoods that we all know to be true even until this day, but I believe we don't research these topics with the technology at our disposal out of fear of hell or somehow offending God. I was always taught it was only two sins that you could not come back from, blasphemy, which is acting against God, and suicide. I began to feel the Bible could not be the true words of God because it had been used for so many evil things. The men of faith in the past gave their blessing for slavery, genocide, and many other atrocities in the name of God.

As I showed earlier, even the people in that time pushed back on the things they were adding to the bible, and one of the reasons the church was split in two in "The Great Schism" in 1054 C.E. The Old Testament in the King James Version has 39 books; that was protocanonical, which means it was accepted early into the Bible without a lot of dispute. Then there were 14 books of the Septuagint that were categorized as deuterocanonical or Apocrypha, which means of doubtful authenticity.

The Septuagint is the Greek translation of the Old Testament from Hebrew sources, and it was assembled around the 3rd century B.C.E. It was assumed to have taken 72 days to translate, using 72 elders, six from each tribe of Israel, but this still debatable. This book is important to this topic because this was also during the Hellenistic or Hellenism, which is understood to mean the spreading of Greek culture over non-Greek people, and existed between 323 B.C.E. until around 300 C.E. During the development of the Septuagint, a letter was written in attempt to explain why it was being made; this document was called Letters of Aristeas (LXX). It explained the people and process it went through during this translation, but never explained what sources they got the information from.

Of the deuterocanonicals or Apocrypha, the books that were left out were Esdras, book of Tobit, book of Judith, book of Wisdom or sometimes called the book of Solomon, book of Sirach or known as Ecclesiasticus, book of Baruch, book of Susanna, which is also found in Daniel, and 1 and 2 Maccabees.

These books were labeled to have been of doubtful authenticity, but were still largely used inside of the doctrine as well as included in the Dead Sea Scrolls and other religious text. They didn't fit the narrative that they wanted to tell, but even in the Bible today we can show where they used large amounts of those books selectively. Notable reformers like Martin Luther were known for opposing a lot of the teachings from the Roman Catholic Church, but we never got details on what these people really believed in and what changes they wanted to make.

Martin Luther wanted to remove the books of Jude, Hebrews, James, and Revelations with the goal to remove scripture that tied salvation to your good works. He lived during the 16th century and following the era of information suppression, information was easy to hide because the majority of the population could not read. Without internet or television, it would take a normal person maybe years to get information from another regions of the world. This gave a lot of validity to myths of that time, when I refer to the word "myth", I am talking about the literal definition, meaning stories containing early history of a people or social phenomenon.

For example, the story of Adam and Eve has been known to be the main origin story of people in the Bible, but the core problem with this story is we know humanity to date back further than the history of the Bible tells us. Another fact of the story that has been long forgotten, changed, or omitted for whatever reason was the fact that Adam was said to have had a wife before Eve by the name of Lilith. This story was widely known in the

Jewish mythology, and Lilith was to have left Adam in the Garden of Eden because she did not want to submit to him. Since the story didn't show a submitting woman, she was demonized and made out to be something evil and eventually turned into a serpent.

The individuals that shaped this story wanted to paint the picture of a perfect woman submitting to the man at every turn, not a woman that had a mind of her own to make choices; she was to be a "helpmate". In my opinion, they took the Lilith story as a threat. Women having power wasn't a part of the system they were trying to put in place, and it would not only upset the social structure but also the authority structure in their households. With the exemption of some women of royal blood, most women of the world had been subject to a permanent state of submission, and they used the Bible to do it. There are a large amount of Bible verses still in the Bible today that go against women having any authority over men. For example, 1 Timothy 2:12: "But I shall not a woman to teach, nor to usurp authority over the man, but to be in silence." There are more like "1 Corinthians 14:34", "1 Corinthians 14:35", "1 Timothy 2:11", and many others describing how women should be silent or submit to the will of man. As we can see, it looks like they turned the evil ex-wife into a snake, and the former independent woman had to go. In the origin story in Genesis, they somehow made everything before making the woman. The Bible has hurt the equal playing field for women, and even in this free country of ours, women didn't receive the right to vote until the 20th century. There are two ways to be fooled, one is to believe what isn't true, and the other is to refuse to believe what is true.

THE MIX UP OF HISTORY

Most history books didn't tell us that the Greeks had a temple inside of Egypt called Naukratis around the 7th century B.C.E., and this temple is one of the reasons you have your Bible today. There were many Greek historians from Thucydides, Arrian, Eusebius, Dionysius, and many others but there was one in particular by the name of Herodotus who was referred to as the father of history and lived between 484-425 B.C.E. Herodotus visited many places like Libya, Babylonia, and Egypt just to name a few and covered an array of topics, as in, recording ancient traditions of the regions he visited, their politics, geography, and conflicts between various cultures looking to take over those lands.

Around this time period in the 5th century B.C.E., Herodotus wrote about all of the different people he met, religions that were being practiced, and any historical accounts from the places he visited and any territorial conflicts taking place. He had famous writings like the "Magnum Opus", which was a description of the Greco-Persian Wars that he called the Histories. Once I read more of Herodotus and his time in Egypt, it wasn't more of what I did find, but more of what I didn't find.

Anyone that been in church for the slightest amount of time or just enjoyed children's cartoon movies like "The Prince of Egypt" has heard the story of Moses and the Exodus and the Hebrews and how they had been enslaved by the Pharaoh during that time. The problem with this story is the historian Herodotus never spoke of Hebrews at all, not in that land or any other around that region, but I wasn't convinced yet so I did more research. Not only was the whole Moses story not documented anywhere but inside of the Bible, but there is no archeological evidence of any large migration of slaves ever exiting Egypt.

Do any other historians place them anywhere around this time? It is very debatable of any real history of Hebrews in Egypt before the invasion of the Greeks. The Moses myth can be also found in similar stories such as "Sargon of Akkad from Mesopotamia", who lived between 2334-2284 B.C.E. The story of Sargon included the same story details as the Moses story, for example: in both myths, they floated a baby down a river in order to escape execution. They also both had the staff of Moses that turned into a serpent, showing the Pharaoh in charge the power of their God so that he would release the supposedly Hebrew people in that land from slavery.

Even in Egypt today, there is no record of any slaves leaving, any plagues of the Bible happening, or any of the events the Bible said went on. Could this all be made up or an "allegory" for something more? You decide. Some may ask why this is important. Moses was supposed to have been the sole author of the Old Testament, and if his story turns out not to be true, then where did the Old Testament come from?

The Moses story flaws don't stop there. During the uprising of the slaves in the 15th century B.C.E., according to the Bible, Ramses is the Pharaoh in charge. The facts of history says the Exodus was around 1446 B.C.E., and during that particular year the Pharaoh was named Thutmose

III , who held the throne from about 1479-1425 B.C.E. The first thing that came to my mind was the similarity between the name Moses and Thutmose, and at first, I thought it was odd. Could this have been an innocent mistake or deliberately changed? And somehow, the Bible leaves out the name Thutmose III.

But I admit it would sound weird if a guy named Moses was fleeing Thutmose, but I will let you make your own assumptions and I will stick to the facts. Herodotus didn't mention any of the events that took place in the Bible, nor did he mention any Hebrews or Jews in any of his work. This should be impossible if they played the role the Bible claims during these times.

Herodotus also covered the pharaohs that were during the times of the events in the Bible, but yet he stills fails to mention or make any reference to any people called Hebrews or Jews. But one people he did speak of was the Hittites and were known to have been black people; they are descendants of Noah that came through his son Ham. Ham was one of Noah's sons to rule over the lands of Southwest Asia, Canaan, which is present day Israel, and Africa, which you can find in Genesis 10:6-20. If you refer to Genesis 9:18-29, you will begin to understand why European bishops would allow this translation, and in those verses it explains the curse of Ham and what they have used as the justification for slavery.

Ham was said to have been cursed and black. He was to be subjected to slavery under his brothers: Japheth, who would reign over the lands of Europe and Asia, and Shem, who ruled over the Middle East, also known as the Shemites. As you can see from the beginning, they have been trying to subject black people to slavery and justify it by the Bible they had made up. To make matters worse, they wrote about how they conquered the lands of black people. For example, Deuteronomy 7:1 says, "When the Lord thy God shall bring thee into the land whither thou goest to possess it, and hath cast out many nations before thee, Hittties, Girgashites, Amorites, Canaanites, and Perizzites, and the Hivites, and the Jebusites, seven nations greater and mightier than thou."

All of those nations the scripture named like Hitties and Jebusites were all black nations according to the Bible because they came from the line of Canaan, which came from the line of Ham as I explained earlier. Even according to the stuff they are trying to create, they cannot hide the fact that they were not the true inhabitants of that land, but the Jebusites or Jebus has no record outside of the

Bible. King David was to have been the ruler around this time, but his whole life and story is very doubtful according to many scholars.

This was just another made-up narrative to fit their plan to dominate black people and eventually the world. As I stated earlier, Ham was over the lands of Canaan, which is present-day Israel. It was also the name of one of his sons, and from the line of Canaan, you get the Hittites. This should give you a little insight on their agenda to inject a Hebrew and Jewish narrative in to fit their Biblical timeline, but neither can be proven in history, nor could they adjust all of the disputes of the Bible.

Herodotus spoke of Hittites on many occasions, explaining their various connections to the land called Israel today. Herodotus writes, "These kingdoms are closely leagued together, and united in the same alliance are their neighbors, the Khatti, or Hittites, who form a great confederacy ruled by a number of petty chiefs, and extended continuously from the boarders of Damascus to the Euphrates at Bir, or Bireh-jik." He described all of those nations as being under the control of Egyptians, not Hebrew or Jews; also the territories he named stretched from present day Israel to present day Iraq.

We know those places today to be inhabited by mainly Arabs or Jews, and this is an example of how history can be changed to favor the victor. In the past when your lands were conquered, they did not only take over the people and political structures, but they also changed the god you worshipped.

Let's give a scenario and say the United States goes to war with China. Somehow China wins, and in our defeat, their soldiers go around destroying all of our churches or converting them to Buddhist temples. Through this process we are no longer allowed to follow, mention, or teach about Christianity, Catholicism, or any other denomination. If you did, you would be anathematized, which means to be cursed or condemned. This may sound crazy, but out of fear of death, how many people you know would choose to convert to Buddhism rather than death?

We must put ourselves in the shoes of the past and realize there were things happening that were out of their control and understand how they might have felt powerless to stop it. Today we have the freedom and the technology to research and fact-check everything we are being told, and everything that I have talked about so far can be easily researched by using the internet.

The fact that Herodotus and every other historian around that time never mentioned Hebrews, the Moses Exodus story, and Jews should bring up great concern if the Bible is something that you believe in to be the true inspired work of God because all of it cannot be explained or relied upon. Ptolemy was responsible for the Septuagint and the Letters of Aristeas (LXX) addressed to his brother Philocrates to explain why they were translating the Hebrew text into Greek, but many scholars agree the letter claims a lot of stuff that still can't be proven to this day.

During the Ptolemy period, they needed a God to unify the Egyptian and Greek people that were cohabitating there, so they created Serapis Christus, which was the sacrificial bull, and Jesus today is the sacrificial lamb.

Many scholars have already established that this was the origin of Jesus Christ, even though he would not make an appearance until the 4th century C.E. You can read more on this subject of ancient Egyptian Gods in books like, The Complete Gods and Goddesses of Ancient Egypt by Richard H. Wilkinson. In the Letters of Aristeas (LXX), it said the Septuagint was translated in 72 days by 72 elders, six from each of the 12 tribes of Israel. Yet it does not tell you who these people are or how they found them; to this day, we don't know who they are.

The religion that is being practiced is Hellenism, which is the culture of Greece and the study or imitation of ancient Greek culture. From between 92-629 C.E., the Romans and Persians were at war over the lands, knowledge, and economical wealth of Africa. The war would end, not in one side being victorious, but in a "status quo ante bellum," which means "the state existing before the war." The term was originally used in treaties to refer to the withdrawal of enemy troops and the restoration of pre-war leadership, but what we didn't know is during this war, new text was being written and passed off as words of God; we now call it the New Testament.

WHAT DO WE DO WITH JESUS?

This was the hardest section of the book to write because Jesus has been the backbone of the black community; no matter what you are going through as long as you believe in him, and that he died on the cross for your sins, you will have everlasting life. He has been exalted to the point I don't think most Christians are able to have an honest conversation about who Jesus really was and the discrepancies in his whole story.

To the world, he is the one man that has ever set foot on planet Earth who had been perfect and supposedly sacrificed himself for the salvation of mankind. As I stated earlier, the Bible has made

Jesus a person with an unmatched or unrivaled power, and whoever believes in him has everlasting life; that is a powerful statement to tell someone that may not be in a good situation and looking for any escape in their life.

I think we all need something to believe in sometimes, but is the "everlasting life" statement true? Or does it just give us a false sense of security? I know you are thinking if we don't believe in the Bible, then what do we believe in? That is something I will get into in a later section. I think it is time to have an honest conversation about who Jesus was, where he came from, and the facts behind his alleged life and death. I will present the main evidence or lack thereof that is used today to try and prove the existence and life of Jesus Christ as we know him today.

You would think the evidence for the existence of Jesus had to be overwhelming because of how many people and religions corroborated his life, but this was not the case at all. I will show how the so-called evidence is either unreliable or minimal at best and how his story could have been used as an allegorical myth; Jesus was just absent from the history all together.

I will demonstrate why Christianity and the belief in Jesus will take more faith than you realize, and the facts just don't add up. The main evidence that is used to support Jesus is the four gospels, Matthew, Mark, Luke, and John as well as various historians such as Flavius Josephus, Pliny the Younger, and Tacitus. They are the few gatekeepers left holding up the Jesus account, but I will explain that they are unreliable and their claims are unsupported; we can't trust them.

I think we all have gotten used to believing in these things as truth because it was passed down; we have realized that generations before us were easily misled, but they did not have the same access to technology nor the freedom to look up the truth that is right in our faces.

The Gospels were supposedly written 40 years after the death of Jesus Christ, which I thought was odd because why wouldn't you written about him while he lived, because obviously we have writing dating back well before the 1st century C.E. In the gospel of Matthew, Ignatius was to have been quoted inside, which means it could have been in circulation as early as 40 C.E. Ignatius of Antioch was known as an early Christian writer and Bishop of Antioch; he died around the year 115 C.E.

The Gospels can be found in other sources like the Codex Sinaticus and the Codex Vaticanus, and between those two books there are 656 differences between just the gospels of Matthew. The Sinaticus was the oldest complete Bible dating back to 330 C.E., but the Vaticanus was the oldest dating back 325 C.E.

The most significant difference between those books or any of the Codex books written in Greek is that none of them mentioned the name Jesus. Some religious people will tell you it's because the Bible was written in Hebrew and that it is older than Greek. This is false and you can see proof in books like, "Hebrew is Greek" by Joseph Yahuda. He proves that both the Aramaic and Hebrew languages derived from Greek, and this is the reason why we don't have evidence of them before the invasion of Egypt by Greece around 332 B.C.E. led by Alexander the Great.

During this time they were making major changes to the so-called holy books and not because God told them to, but for selfish and worldly reasons. The gospel of Matthew uses Mark as a roadmap, just adding and clarifying events that were already stated. For example, Matthew 24:15 and Mark 13:14 say virtually the same thing. For more examples, you can refer to Matthew 9:6, Mark 2:10, and Luke 5:24, and also Matthew 27:18 and Mark 15:10. For the gospels to have come from different authors, translated from different languages, and written in different periods, they have a lot of striking similarities.

Matthew has 1,068 verses with 18,293 words, and around 60% of it can be found in the gospel of Mark. Mark is known to be the earliest of all of the four gospels, and it was used in the creation of most of the information in the gospel of Matthew; as I stated earlier, over 50% can be found within its pages. Mark is said to be the oldest largely because it is the shortest of the four gospels with 661 verses with 11,025 words, not only for that reason, but because 97% of Mark is duplicated inside the writings of Matthew and 88% inside of Luke. As I stated earlier, only 60% of Matthew and 47% of Luke is found in Mark which indicates Mark came first.

Now that we have established that Mark was the first gospel created according to the evidence, we must state that he was not an eye witness for the account, but retold the teachings of Peter. Mark was a disciple and this was said to have taken place between 55-70 C.E, and has around 567 changes between the Codex Sinaticus and the Codex Vaticanus manuscripts.

My question was if the first account for the existence of Jesus wasn't an eye witness, how can it or the other be trusted? Mark also doesn't mention the birth of Jesus, Sermon on the Mount, Lord's Prayer, resurrection appearances by Jesus, and the list continues. We must remember none of the accounts or events happening in the gospels can be found outside of the Bible or in any historical documents found today.

The Gospel of Luke is in the same boat as the others with 791 differences between the Codex Sinaticus and Codex Vaticanus. Luke was not an eye witness either, or even his companion Paul, but was said to have spoken to an eye witness; you can refer to this even in the Bible in Luke 1:2. Luke has 1,149 verses and 19,376 words, but yet fails to mention noteworthy events. As you can see from gospel to gospel, there are the same unreliable accounts from unknown eye witnesses; it's just hard for me to believe in all of the stories when history clearly shows these things never took place. The gospel of John takes the gold with over one thousand differences between the Codex Sinaticus and Codex Vaticanus. John was also a victim of countless additions, and the original manuscript of John ended at John 5:4. One of the most notable quotes from pastors is John 8:7, "He that is without sin cast the first stone." Sadly this is a later addition.

John was known to be anonymous, and many scholars agree that John is written significantly different from Matthew, Mark, or Luke, but it's still highly debated. John did the same as the other and used the already written manuscripts as a guide while adding his own personal touch; you can see proof of this by comparing verses like John 6 and Mark 6, John 18 and Mark 14, and many others.

We just have to want to see the contradictions that are in front of us. While reading the gospels, you will read the word "multitude", which simply means a large number, and usually describing the following that Jesus may have had. It's hard to agree with that definition of the description towards Christians or Jesus because they had somehow still managed to not be mentioned outside of the Bible.

The Gospel of John also made up characters that were never mentioned anywhere else ever before by the name of Lazarus and Nicodemus; these were people not mentioned in any of the other gospels or anywhere outside of the Bible, but yet supposedly had appearances in the life of Jesus.

Lazarus was known to be a follower of Jesus, and Jesus was said to have been the one who brought him back from the dead. Movies have been made with the same plot in mind, for example, "The Lazarus Effect." Nicodemus is first mentioned in

John and was said to have met with Jesus at night and may have helped with his burial. Jesus was said to have lived between 4 and 36 C.E. around the time of Pontius Pilot. Some of the historians that documented that period, regional conflict, or similar topics were Pliny the Younger (61-113 C.E.), Tacitus who lived between (54-120 C.E.), and Suetonius that lived between (69-130 C.E.).

Suetonius wrote on multiple subjects, but one of his most noticeable works was "Life of Claudius", "Life of Nero", and his early Christian writings. Most of Suetonius' writings that were supposed to coincide with the life of Jesus fail to even mention the name Jesus Christ. The reference that scholars try to draw from Suetonius to prove the existence of Jesus does not give proof that a historical man by the name of Jesus walked this earth. Tacitus also wrote on similar topics, but somehow never mentions the name Jesus, only the name of "Christus" being put to death by Pontius Pilate in the reign of Tiberius, which is mentioned only once in the entire Bible in Luke 3:1.

As I explained earlier, the term Christus or Christ is a common term used to describe anyone of deity status. Tiberius and many others can't be found in early Christian writings in the first 150 years after Jesus was to have supposedly died.

I want you to realize how vague and undescriptive some of the references they have used as irrefutable evidence for Jesus; they don't actually show any actual proof, but I will leave it up to you to make your own assumptions. If Jesus and Christians had the multitude of followers they claimed to have had, why they were missed all through real history? What it claims can only be found within its own pages and nowhere else. As a comedian once stated, "If Jesus was a carpenter, why did they not keep any of his work?" Sounded a bit silly at the time, but it actually makes a lot of sense. In the phony passage in the Antiquities of the Jews by Josephus called the "Testimonium Flavianum", there is another pathetic reference to prove the existence of Jesus Christ; there is also a short passage in the works of the Roman historian Pliny the Younger.

> *"The worshippers of Serapis are Christians, and those are devoted to the God Serapis, who call themselves the bishops of Christ. There is no ruler of a Jewish synagogue, no Samaritan, no Presbyter of the Christians, who is not either an astrologer, a soothsayer, or a minister to obscene pleasures. The very Patriarch himself, should he come into Egypt, would be required by some to worship Serapis,*

and by others to worship Christ. They have, however, but one God, and it is one and the self-same whom Christians, Jews and Gentiles alike adore."

As you can see the quote they try to use has no reference to a man named Jesus, but is constantly used to without a doubt prove the life and death of an earthly Jesus. Seneca the Younger lived between (4 B.C.E.-65 C.E.) and served as a Roman Stoic Philosopher; Stoicism dominated the philosophy during the Hellenistic period. Seneca wrote about people like Claudius, who was a Roman Emperor, Nero, and the Roman regions, but still no mention of Jesus, or any multitude of Christians being persecuted by the government.

I can quote person after person that failed to mention Jesus Christ and the evidence is overwhelming. I believe if we put more time, money, and efforts into ourselves rather than turning to a mystical figure, we would all be in a better place. The last historical person I will name is Philo of Alexander, who also went by Philo Judaeus. He was a Hellenistic Jewish Philosopher that lived between 25 B.C.E. to 50 C.E., and he was also an Embassy from the Jews Court of Emperor Gaius Caligula. He spent time in Jerusalem and wrote on the subjects of Jewish religion and contemporary politics.

With all of these great accomplishments, he was in the right regions around the correct time but somehow misses the life and death of the faith's lord and savior. Philo was in the correct place around the right time and wrote in the very subject that should have captured the historical story of Jesus, nor does he verify any of the stories said to have happened during that time. One can only assume from its absence that it may not have happened.

I can give examples on how much the evidence of Jesus and how most of the claims in the Bible can't be proven, but that's not the purpose of this book. My goal was to give you enough foundation to begin to do your own research, and maybe then you will seek the truth and the real inner power these religions speak of; expose this bible we have today in the light of truth.

Where Do We Go from Here?

I have contemplated on where we go from here and what people should believe in. Do you no longer believe in the stories or the characters of the Bible? I realize this is an impossible question to answer because it is something each person has to figure out for themselves. If you want to take the lessons out of the Bible, we need to pay more attention to the scriptures that teach of inner power and the temple of God being within us.

For example, 1 Corinthians 3:16-17 and Acts 17:24. Most of us have spent our entire lives being told and taught what other people think we should believe in and that's fine until we run into a road block, then who do we turn to? The normal answer would be God or Jesus, but my answer would be to look for the power within and seek out what makes you happy.

Most of the people we see today that are millionaires and enjoy what they do is because they turned what they enjoyed into what they do, and not what they do into what they enjoy. It may have been life or death for past black people to believe in a historical Jesus; I can't really say because those were extreme circumstances. But today I can say Jesus has become a scheme to manipulate poor communities, take the few dollars they do have while allowing the neighborhoods around them to fall apart.

The church has become a race to see who can fill the biggest arena around the nation, put out feel-good stories while not addressing the root problem of society, and listening to the most notable pastors say things like poverty is not the church's problem. If we need somewhere to go on Sundays to fill the time, how about we start a neighborhood group and share business ideas or anything that will help us in our future? Rather than give your money to the church with no accountability or restraints, so the pastor can travel easier in his private jet.

I do not think every pastor is in that boat, but I could not be a pastor at a church pulling in millions, but yet have members that struggle daily just to get by? The neighborhoods of their members have become a ground for forever renters and never ownership. Most of the religious text we have today as I demonstrated has been manipulated and changed for purposes other than to do the will of God.

Dating back to the earliest sources we get the Bible, we see it being changed to fit the single-mindedness of whoever was ruling at the time. The Greeks began deculturalization, which meant they forced people of another land to worship their pagan Gods and take on the Greek way of life; this began with the invasion of the Greeks and Alexander the Great in 332 B.C.E.

The Septuagint and the Hellenistic religion along with Serapis Christus was made to control the Egyptian people at that time, which was widely followed from the 4th century B.C.E. and the Council of Nicea in 325 C.E. All of the codex manuscripts found written in Greek like the Codex Sinaticus, Codex Vaticanus, Codex Alexandrinus, and many others never mentioned the name of Jesus Christ.

As I showed, there were a significant amount of differences among the translations, which tells me they can't possibly be trusted. I must admit I do not write, speak, or read Greek, but I do know what the name Jesus Christ looks like in Greek, and through all of the pages I went through, they did not mention his name once, even in the exact scriptures. He is mentioned in the King James Bible, but his name remains absent in the correlated Greek text that this doctrine was copied from. Scholars could only point to unrelated abbreviations that were never seen more than once in the place for Jesus.

This can only mean that the name of Jesus was added into the doctrine during a later time in history; I pointed out earlier the religious leaders of that time added him in at the Council of Nicea in 325 C.E. We have been deceived through movies and other social constructs without knowing it. For instance, the false perception of the number in sequence "666" we all know to be a sign of evil, but in reality it is the numbers of life for melanated people and the genetic code for human DNA representing 6 protons, 6 neutrons, and 6 electrons.

We have to re-examine all of our history even in this country because I am beginning to believe it was a lot more black people in this country when Columbus got here than they are telling us, but that is a subject for another book. If you think about it, we have been taught to hate ourselves. It says it in the Bible in verses like Revelations 13:18. "This call for wisdom: let the one who has understanding calculate the number of the beast, for it is the number of a man, and his number is 666."

The book of Revelations was not added until the 5th century C.E. and also not found anywhere else or referenced outside of the Bible. We also explored the historians and people documenting the period like Herodotus, Pliny the Younger, Suetonius, Tacitus, Seneca the Younger, Flavius Josephus, and Philo of Alexandria, just to name a few; none of them mentioned the name Jesus or spoke any detail about him. The books of the Bible, like the original Psalms of David, were really the work of the Egyptian Pharaoh Akhenaten, who died around 1335 B.C.E. This was hundreds of years before King David ever lived, so whose words are they?

The four gospels: Matthew, Mark, Luke, and John, which are majorly used for the existence of Jesus, were not eyewitnesses as I explained. They were written at least 40 years after he was to have supposedly lived, and they used each other's work as a guide to write their gospels. I showed how through time how the Bible was influenced to serve the needs of the greedy, suppress the rights of the mass population, and kill in the name of God.

I came to the conclusion that knowledge is the key to enlightenment, and as long as we always seek to know the truth, it is hard to be deceived. Ironically, the Bible has over a hundred verses talking about how good knowledge is, but punishes Adam for seeking to eat from the tree of knowledge. Are these stories of the Bible contradictory, or are these stories an allegory for events happening during that time?

The whole story of Jesus is suspected to be an allegory for the yearly journey of the Sun passing through each of the 12 zodiac signs, or 12 disciples, every 25th day of December; the winter solstice going on during that time that requires the Sun to disappear for three days and rise again. According to the Bible and scholars, it is unclear what month Jesus was born in, but most agree it was not in December as we all celebrate today.

We have to remember, no matter how bad we want Jesus to have existed, and no matter how much we think he has done for our lives, it doesn't make him real. I hope this gives individuals the power to take control over their lives and research everything.

Even the things we have been taught from our parents and teachers need research because we all could have been misled. I have come to the conclusion that I do not want my kids to know Jesus or the Bible other than to expand their knowledge of the world around them. I don't want them to know the hurt of believing in something you will never be able to prove is the true work of God. I don't want them believing in a religion not worthy of their devotion. I don't want them to feel excluded because a book has told them that they are inferior and subjected to a life of slavery. I don't want them to give their time and money to something that doesn't plan to give back.

I just don't. Most people will assume that I wrote this book out of hate, hate for the Bible or religion in general, but they would be wrong. This book was written out of love. The reason is that I love myself and my people too much to learn the truth of something we have followed our whole life and not want to share it with the world.

I feel the love I have inside has been betrayed by the beliefs I have been taught my whole life; and if you love someone, I believe you should give them the knowledge that can possibly set them free. There are millions of people being hurt and misled by the religions we have today.

I don't believe everyone that has faith in religion is misled; they may know the truth but refuse to say it because it is unpopular. It might ruin whatever is going on in their life, politically or otherwise, and many just don't care, which can be an even worse problem. You can't find the graves of any of the characters in the Bible, or the Koran, or the Tanakh, or even Torah, for that matter.

These are the things that people don't talk about, but can be easily verified by using the internet; none of these characters from religious text can be verified with physical evidence. All over the world we can find remains of African culture that dates back before the time of Jesus or Moses, but yet the individuals we heard about in religious text have yet to be found. We must ask ourselves why? I don't expect everyone to read every book that I read in order to put this book together, but hopefully this will give you a foundation of knowledge and courage in order to seek out the truth for yourself. I am confident you may start to see things in a whole new light.

About the Author
Lloyd C. Ford, II

A devoted Houston native received a B.B.A in management information systems from Prairie View A&M University. He is a neighborhood leader and is passionate about community and economic growth of others. Lloyd is a technically skilled, educated professional who brings progressive and practical knowledge in Information Technology. As a proactive team player with proven leadership skills, Lloyd has the ability to develop and inspire others through his leadership and dedication.

He is serving the community by feeding the homeless and has volunteered for programs such as Meals on Wheels. Through his countless efforts and persistent drive, Lloyd believes in promoting positive community and economic growth in the Houston community for all. "There is nothing better than adversity. Every defeat, every heartbreak, every loss contains its own seed, its own lesson on how to improve your performance next time."

www.ingramcontent.com/pod-product-compliance
Lightning Source LLC
Chambersburg PA
CBHW070937160426
43193CB00011B/1716